Bible Story Games
for Preschoolers

Loveland, Colorado

Bible Story Games for Preschoolers

Copyright © 1998 Group Publishing, Inc.

Credits
Contributing Authors: Donna L. Alexander, Joy B. Cole, Mary Ann Craven, Nanette Goings, Sheila A. Halasz, Ellen Javernick, Reverend Mike Morris, Barbie Murphy, Ken Niles, Nancy Paulson, and Dave Thornton
Book Acquisitions Editor: Beth Rowland Wolf
Editor: Lori Haynes Niles
Creative Development Editor: Dave Thornton
Chief Creative Officer: Joani Schultz
Copy Editor: Julie Meiklejohn
Art Director: Kari K. Monson
Cover Art Director: Jeff A. Storm
Computer Graphic Artist: Joyce Douglas
Cover Designer: Elise Lansdon
Cover Photographer: Jafe Parsons and PhotoDisc
Illustrator: Ben Mahan
Production Manager: Peggy Naylor

Library of Congress Cataloging-in-Publication Data
Bible story games for preschoolers.
     p.   cm.
   Includes index.
   ISBN 0-7644-2059-3
   1. Christian education of preschool children. 2. Bible games and puzzles. I. Group Publishing.
     BV1475.7.B53   1998
     268' .432–dc21   97-52258
                                                CIP

10 9 8 7 6 5 4 3 2 1   07 06 05 04 03 02 01 00 99 98

Printed in the United States of America.

Contents

96896

John

Stories Jesus Told 83

The Early Church .98

Introduction

· ·

Preschoolers love to play! *And* **that's how they learn best.**

Bible Story Games for Preschoolers will help children's minds
lock in a portion of God's Word through a fun experience. The
games in this book will give your preschoolers a chance to
develop important social skills, such as cooperating, taking turns, listening, and following directions. You'll provide children age-appropri-
ate challenges to help build their confidence, and because the games
are noncompetitive, everyone feels like a winner every time!

Many of the games offer suggestions for tailoring to your
class. Feel free to simplify any game for your youngest preschoolers
or jazz it up to challenge older children. Keep the tone upbeat, and
cheer for each child as kids all learn from God's Word!

Here are some age-level characteristics to keep in mind as you
plan for fun:

● Two-year-olds move with lots of energy but they lack coordination,
so keep the movements simple. Two-year-olds may be shy about doing
an activity, but they will be quite eager if you join them. So hold their
hands as they walk to a goal line, or take time to show an individual how
to do an action even if you already modeled it for the group. Adapt
games so that there is very little (if any!) waiting for these little ones by
using multiple game supplies so they can all participate at once. The key
word for their teachers is **encourage, encourage, encourage!**

● Three- and four-year-olds have lots of energy. Keep things moving
for these powerhouses! Involve them in the game even if it isn't their
turn by encouraging them to watch, cheer, or remember key facts
about the Bible story as they wait. Help them develop group-play skills
by stopping a game while they are still having fun so that you keep
within their attention span. Then play the game again if there is an interest. The key word for their teachers is **cheer, cheer, cheer!**

● Five-year-olds are learning to strategize and are enthusiastic
game players. They may want to "win" but are easily devastated if
they lose, so stress participation and working together. When they are
pretending to be Bible characters, they are likely to bring the house
down with their dramatic flair, so let them embellish games with new
twists. These children thrive on knowing they have the approval of
others. The key word for their teachers is **praise, praise, praise.**

Enjoy the games in this book. As you play, you'll be part of
building the lifelong perception that getting into God's Word is one
of the most fun challenges around!

Genesis

Creation Secrets

Supplies: A sheet; several paper bags; items found in nature such as a pine cone, a rock, dirt, a flower, leaves or grass, an acorn, or a piece of fruit

Scripture: Genesis 1

Energy Level: Low

Use this game to help children get in touch with God's creation.

Spread the sheet out on the floor. Have the children sit in a circle around the sheet. Place the paper bags in the center of the circle.

Say: **God made the world and everything in it. Some of God's creations are hidden inside these bags. When I bring a bag to you, reach in without looking. Make a guess about what's in the bag, and keep your guess a secret.**

Coach's Comment

Put each of your nature items in a separate paper bag, and set the bags out ahead of time.

Walk around the inside of the circle, and let each child reach in the bag to feel. You may need to reassure individuals that nothing in the bag will hurt them. After everyone has felt the object inside the bag, empty it on the sheet in the center of the circle and have everyone yell out what was inside.

Allow a few seconds of congratulations and then say: **When everyone is ready, we will pass around the next bag.**

Work through the bags one at a time until all the objects have been identified.

For more fun, turn the items into a nature montage you can hang in your classroom.

Ring Around Creation

Supplies: A long cord or a piece of heavy string (about one foot per child), a ring that will pass over the cord (such as a wooden craft-loop or a steel washer), a cassette player, and a lively music tape

Scripture: Genesis 1–2

Energy Level: Medium

This game gives kids a lively way to recall the Creation story.

Place the ring on the string, and tie the string into a loop. Have the children stand shoulder to shoulder in a circle, and hand them the string with the ring on it to hold.

Say: **Let's take backward steps to spread out as far as we can so the string is tight.** Count steps backward until the children are far enough apart so that the string is taut but not stretched enough to risk breaking. Say: **We'll push the ring around on the string as fast as we can while the music is playing. If you have the ring in front of you when I stop the music, you will tell something that you remember God made when he was creating the world. Then we'll start the music again and push the ring around the string until the music stops again. We'll play until everyone has had a turn.**

Animal Action

Supplies: None

Scripture: Genesis 2:19-20

Energy Level: Medium

Kids will enjoy becoming Adam's new zoo.

Seat children in a group so that all of them can see you.

Say: **Let's pretend that I'm Adam and that you're the animals God made. God has given me the job of naming you. I'm going to choose one person to turn around and step away from the group so he or she won't hear what animal I am telling the rest of you to be. That person will be the guesser. When I say out loud, "One, two, three; guess which animal we might be!" everyone in the group will start acting like the animal I told you to be. Then the guesser is going to turn around and try to guess what animal you are.**

Coach's Comment

To help you think quickly on your feet, write out a list of animals before the game.

Whisper the same animal name in each child's ear. Say the rhyme, and let the children act out the animal until the guesser identifies it. After the first child has guessed, choose other children until each child has had a turn. Try having the guesser become the new Adam. Be ready to help the child choose another animal and say the rhyme.

To make the game more challenging, encourage older kids to act out each animal silently. Younger children will enjoy the game more (and be more easily identified) if they also make animal sounds.

The Big Snake

Supplies: Masking tape

Scripture: Genesis 3

Energy Level: High

Play this game after you have told about how the cunning Serpent tricked Eve in the Garden of Eden.

Place a line of masking tape on one side of the room to be the line between the beautiful Garden of Eden and the outside world. Say: **In the Bible, a big snake tricked Eve. After that, God would never let him go into the beautiful garden he lived in again. Today we're going to make a big snake that wiggles and hisses around the room. We'll start by making little snakes and then we'll all hook together to make one big snake.**

Have the children start by stretching out on the floor on their tummies. Have them practice slithering on their own. When they feel comfortable doing that, help each child choose a partner. (Young preschoolers will enjoy moving on to the obstacle stage without hooking up to partners.)

Show children how one person can hold the ankles of a partner to make a two-person snake that slithers across the floor on its belly. Then have children connect to make four-person snakes. Continue in this manner until the whole group is one big snake. Depending on your kids' ability, you can set up obstacles so the giant snake can crawl over "mountains" and through "holes" in a path to the end of the garden. Once the children cross over the tape line, the game is over.

The Animal Race

Supplies: A piece of rope or a board for a tightrope, a blanket draped over a table or two chairs for a tunnel, paper-circle steppingstones for crossing a river, two chairs put together for a mountain, a table on its side for an ark, and a spray bottle filled with water

Scripture: Genesis 6, 7, and 8

Energy Level: High

Bring the story of Noah and the ark to life in this awesome obstacle course.

Say: **When Noah had to get all the animals on the ark, some of them must have had to travel a long way to get there on time. Today we'll travel the way some of them did to get safely on the ark.**

Explain the course to the children as you build it. Lay the rope or board on the floor, and identify it as a long tree branch to climb over. Drape the blanket over a table or two chairs, and tell the kids it's a cave to climb through. Place the paper circles as steppingstones to help children cross a wide river. Put two chairs together back-to-back to make a tall mountain to climb. Show the tipped-over table that will be the ark.

Lead the children through the course from beginning to end, misting them all with water as they climb into the ark. Then let one of the kids pick an animal, and have everyone try the course again as that animal. Once everyone has had a chance to choose an animal, let all the kids make their favorite animal noises from inside the ark!

Rainbow Ball

Supplies: A bag of cotton batting, string or tape, a sock, thumbtacks, and long strips of rainbow-colored ribbon or crepe paper

Scripture: Genesis 9:12-16

Energy Level: Medium

Create your own rainbows to remind kids that God always keeps his promises.

Push a handful of cotton batting into the toe of the sock. You should have a somewhat firm ball. Tie a knot in the sock just above the batting. Use string or tape to attach crepe paper or ribbons to the other end of the sock, making a ball with streamers. Suspend the remainder of the batting from the ceiling by tying several pieces of string around it and then tacking the ends of the string to the ceiling. This "cloud" should hang just a bit higher than the children's heads.

Have the children stand on one side of the cloud. Show them how the ball creates a rainbow when it is thrown up and over the cloud above their heads. Each child may take a turn moving to the other side of the cloud and throwing the ball over the cloud to someone he or she selects from the group. This catcher becomes the thrower in the next round. The thrower may return to the group after his or her turn. Teach the children this rhythmic chant they can repeat together each time the thrower throws:

> **Promises, promises—**
> **God always keeps his promises**
> > **To Noah and to** (insert the name of the child the thrower has selected to catch the ball).

Play until each child has had a turn throwing and catching.

Oh, No! Look Out Below!

Supplies: Several sets of small blocks. (Try to have one set for every three to four children.)

Scripture: Genesis 11:1-9

Energy Level: Medium

Kids will play this simple game over and over after hearing the story of the Tower of Babel.

Arrange the room so that each group of three to four children has plenty of floor space. Give each group a set of blocks.

Say: **Remember the story of the men who thought they would build a tower high enough to reach heaven? God did not let them finish the tower because he wanted the men to understand that believing in him is the only way to heaven. Today we're going to build towers, too. Our towers won't reach heaven either. They'll fall to the ground when they get too high.** Let the kids play for several minutes, working together to build the biggest tower they can.

Next, start a new tower and show children how to place the blocks so that it's difficult to get the *next* block to balance. Have them carefully continue to add new blocks until the tower wobbles and falls. As they anticipate the tower falling, have the kids shout out the warning "Oh, no! Look out below!" Let the person who placed the last block place the first one in the next round.

Abram's Amblings

Supplies: A box or a small suitcase and a bag containing a few things to pack, such as clothing, a toothbrush, and shampoo

Scripture: Genesis 12:1-5

Energy Level: High

Kids will join Abram in his journey from Haran to the land of Canaan.

Say: **What do you take with you when you go on a trip with your family?** Wait for the children to give answers. As they mention the things you have in the bag, pull them out and load them into the suitcase or box.

Say: **We're going to pretend we're traveling with Abram and his family. Let's take our suitcase and move to a new country!**

Form two groups of children, and put a group at each end of the play area. Have group members line up single file. Give one group the suitcase. The first child in line will carry the suitcase to the other group, who will receive it and send the group member at the head of its line back to the other side carrying the suitcase. Repeat the traveling back and forth until each child on each team has had a chance to carry the suitcase. To add challenge and excitement, ask each child to empty the contents of the suitcase when he or she arrives at the other side. Direct the next traveler to repack the suitcase before traveling back.

Give a Little, Take a Lot

Supplies: Masking tape or chairs
Scripture: Genesis 13
Energy Level: Medium

Sharpen kids' observation skills in this game based on the story of Abram and Lot dividing the land.

Place a line of tape or a row of chairs at the front of the class to separate Lot's land and Abram's land. Say: **The Bible tells us that Abram and Lot divided up land so they would each have their own place to live. Abram let Lot choose which land he wanted first. Today you're going to be the land they divided. I'll be Lot, and one of you will be Abram.** Choose a child to be Abram, and have him or her stand at the front of the class next to you on the other side of the tape line. Say: **Listen carefully to what I say so that you'll know whether you're part of my land or Abram's land. If you're part of my land, come sit in front of me. If you're part of Abram's land, sit in front of our friend, Abram.**

Say: **I, Lot, will take everyone who is wearing stripes. Abram will say: "I'll take everyone who is not wearing stripes."** Let Abram repeat after you.

Encourage children to move to the proper sides of the room. When the class has divided, choose another Abram and decide on a different feature to divide the class by. Some possible features to use are tennis shoes/no tennis shoes, shoelaces/no shoelaces, buttons/no buttons, wearing red/not wearing red.

Continue as long as the kids are interested.

Rebekah's Water Relay

Supplies: Paper cups and a pitcher of water

Scripture: Genesis 24

Energy Level: High

Quench a powerful thirst as Rebekah waters the camels in this fun relay.

Choose one of the children to be Rebekah, and have her stand near the water and cups on one side of the room. Choose another child to be Abraham's servant, and have him stand on the opposite side of the room. Have the other children be camels by getting down on all fours and forming a line behind Abraham's servant.

Have Abraham's servant step away from the camels to Rebekah and say, "May I have some water, please?" After Rebekah hands the servant a cup, she should say, "Let me give your camels a drink." The first camel will race across the room on all fours to drink a fresh cup of water. The first camel will race back to touch the next camel on the shoulder so he or she can get a drink, and so on. When all the camels are finished, Abraham's servant will yell, "Thank you, Rebekah!"

Coach's Comment

Pour glasses of water ahead of time and set them on a table, ready for "Rebekah" to hand out.

Blind Blessings

Supplies: A blindfold

Scripture: Genesis 27

Energy Level: Low

Use this game to help children learn about their sense of touch and how they can find out about people or things without using their eyes.

Help children sit in a circle facing the center.

Ask: **What do you notice about the people in our class? Who has short hair? Long hair? Who has a bow in her hair?**

Coach's Comment

Always offer young children the choice of wearing a blindfold or closing their eyes tightly. Sometimes a stretchy headband or wrist-band works better than a traditional blindfold.

Say: **Isaac was blind, but he thought he could discover which of his sons was with him by the hair he felt. Let's see how well we can do figuring out who someone is by touching his or her hair.**

Select one person to be Jacob and Esau's father, Isaac. Have Isaac sit on a chair in the center of the circle, and blindfold him or her. Select another child to come near Isaac and see if Isaac can guess the person's identity by gently touching his or her hair and clothing. If Isaac is having difficulty guessing correctly, ask the other children to give some clues. Take turns until everyone has had the opportunity to be either Isaac or the other child.

Joseph's Journey

Supplies: Masking tape, a rope, a broom, a chair, and a paper crown

Scripture: Genesis 37–45

Energy Level: Medium

Kids will walk in Joseph's footsteps down this winding road.

Before beginning this game, set up a winding course consisting of one four-foot strip of masking tape, followed by a circle made with a rope, then a broom, and finally a chair with a paper crown sitting on it. Make the stations far enough apart so that the children have to take several steps between stations. Have kids line up single file before the first station.

Say: **Let's walk through Joseph's life together. Listen closely, and I will teach you a verse to say as you walk through the course.** (This verse can be sung with each line going one note up the scale.)

Joseph walked a long way *(walk on the masking tape)*;
Got thrown into a well. *(Jump into the rope circle, and crouch down.)*
His brothers didn't like him *(shake your head, and make taunting faces)*,
As anyone could tell!
He worked for Egypt's rulers *(sweep with the broom)*;
Got thrown into a jail. *(Crouch down behind the chair.)*
But he became a ruler *(put the crown on)*,
'Cause God can never fail! *(Throw up both arms.)*

Demonstrate the relay course. Put the crown back on the chair, and walk back to the tape line. Shake the hand of the first person in line. Say: **The handshake shows that Joseph and his brothers finally got back together again, which made them all very happy.**

Say: **Now we will begin the game with the first person in line doing just what I showed you. After you have walked back to the beginning of the line and shaken the next person's hand, go to the end of the line. Then the next person in line may take his or her turn to go on Joseph's journey.**

Play until everyone has had a turn.

The Beautiful Coat

Supplies: A coat, at least one crepe paper streamer for each child (multicolored streamers are best), and at least one spring-hinged clothespin for each child

Scripture: Genesis 37

Energy Level: Low

In this game, kids will create a representation of Joseph's special coat.

Have the kids sit in a tight semicircle with the streamers and clothespins in the center and the coat laid out on the floor a few feet away from the group. Say: **Joseph had lots of brothers, but there was only one special coat. Today, each of you will get a chance to wear the beautiful coat we are going to decorate!** Have each child hold out one fist. Tap a child's hand on each phrase of the following poem:

One brother,	Decorate the coat
Two brothers,	That's sitting
Three brothers,	On the floor!
Four—	

Let the child whose fist is tapped on the last line select a piece of crepe paper and use the clothespin to attach it to the coat. Children may need help opening the clothespins. Have the child rejoin the group without putting his or her fist out to be tapped again. Children can repeat the poem with you as you continue until each child has had a turn.

Repeat the same process with this verse:

Four brothers,	Try on
Three brothers,	The coat
Two brothers,	Just for
One—	Fun!

Help the child whose fist is touched put the decorated coat on and model it. Lead the children in admiring the beautiful coat as each child models. Continue until each child has had a turn.

The Israelites

Moses on the River

Supplies: A box, blankets, a doll, and masking tape

Scripture: Exodus 2

Energy Level: High

This is an action-packed game to reinforce that God protected baby Moses in the Nile.

Place the doll and the blankets in the box to represent baby Moses in the basket. Have the children stand all over the room so that no one is close enough to touch another person without moving. The kids are reeds in the Nile River. Place a crooked or zigzag line of tape across the room.

Remind the children that the river was a dangerous place where God protected baby Moses. Have an older child or a helper walk back and forth on the tape line (at a predictable pace), opening and closing his or her arms in rhythm like a crocodile mouth. Show the children how to push the box from one person to another and then sit down, so you can tell they've had turns. Their job is to push the baby from reed to reed, keeping him away from the crocodile. When all the children are seated, the whole group should shout and cheer, "The baby has been found!"

Plague Play

Supplies: Red fabric (a sheet, a towel, or a blanket) and soft balls or paper wads

Scripture: Exodus 7–11

Energy Level: High

Get ready for fun as your preschoolers *become* the plagues of Egypt.

Say: Today we will see what God did to show Pharaoh who was really the King. When Moses told Pharaoh to let the Israelites go, Pharaoh said "no" ten times. Let's act out the ten miracles God did to show Pharaoh that God was the King. **First, God turned Aaron's stick into a snake.** Have the children lay down on their stomachs and wiggle like snakes. Say: **Second, God turned the river into blood.** Have the children wave the red fabric up and down like a river current. Say: **Third, God sent frogs to cover the land.** Have the children hop up and down like frogs. Say: **Fourth, God filled the air with gnats.** Have the children wave their arms like they're swatting gnats. Say: **Fifth, God let the cows die all at once.** Have the children stand on all fours and then fall down on the count of three. Say: **Sixth, God gave the people sores all over their bodies.** Have the children hop up and down and yell "ouch!" Say: **Seventh, he sent hail falling down from the sky.** Have the children throw the soft balls or paper wads up into the air. Say: **Eighth, he sent a swarm of locusts to cover the land.** Have the children hop on all fours while chomping with their mouths. Say: **Ninth, he turned the daylight into darkness.** Have the children close their eyes for a few seconds. Say: **Tenth, he allowed some Egyptian children to die, but he protected all the Hebrew children.** Have the children clap and cheer.

After resting for a moment, repeat the plagues more rapidly. Try it in slow motion for even more fun.

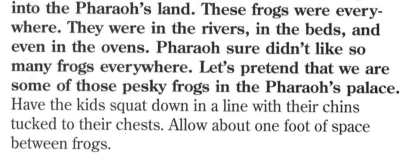

Pharaoh's Frogs

Supplies: None

Scripture: Exodus 8:1-15

Energy Level: High

Children will fly high in this leapfrog game to use with the story of Egypt's plague of the frogs.

This game works best in the middle of a large room, or, better yet, outside. Frogs love cool grass, you know.

Say: **In this Bible story, Pharaoh wouldn't let Moses and his people leave the country. So God sent many frogs into the Pharaoh's land. These frogs were everywhere. They were in the rivers, in the beds, and even in the ovens. Pharaoh sure didn't like so many frogs everywhere. Let's pretend that we are some of those pesky frogs in the Pharaoh's palace.** Have the kids squat down in a line with their chins tucked to their chests. Allow about one foot of space between frogs.

Coach's Comment

To make sure this game runs smoothly, have two adults ready to "spot" your "frogs."

Have the last frog in the line hold on to the hands of two helpers. Helpers will need to squat and stand with the jumper as he or she jumps over each frog. Children will need varying degrees of help. When the first jumper has finished the line, he or she becomes a frog at the front of the line. Use this chant to help pace the children and make it easier to spot them:

Jump, jump, jump, jump, jump *(say "jump" for each child in line);*
The frogs made Pharaoh quite a grump!

Run, Run, as Fast as You Can

Supplies: Two long pieces of rope or yarn

Scripture: Exodus 14

Energy Level: High

Follow the story of the crossing of the Red Sea with this energy-burning game.

Show the children the ropes representing the walls of water that separated at God's command. Teach this refrain that children will shout to the Egyptian soldiers: **Run, run, as fast as you can. You can't catch us. We're part of God's plan.** Pick three volunteers to help you be the first rope-holders. Select one or two children to start as the soldiers and one child to be Moses. The rest of the children will be the Israelites. Start the game with all the escaping Israelites lined up behind Moses. Have the soldiers stand at the end of the line.

Say: **When Moses leads you to the ropes, he'll tell the Red Sea to separate. The rope holders will move the ropes away from each other. The Israelites will run between the ropes, shouting to the soldiers, "Run, run, as fast as you can. You can't catch us. We're part of God's plan." Just as the soldiers begin to run between the ropes, the rope holders will bring the ropes together and catch the soldiers.**

Have children change roles after each game. After you've played the game a couple of times, let Moses decide what method of locomotion his people should take (hopping, skipping, and crawling are a few possibilities). Change the refrain accordingly, and let the kids change roles frequently.

Moses Leads His People

Supplies: A carpet square or a towel and a music source.

Scripture: Exodus

Energy Level: Medium

This game will fit with any part of the story of Moses leading God's people.

Place the carpet square or towel in the center of your play area. Have the children form a line. The leader is Moses. Tell Moses he or she can take any route around the room as long as he or she keeps the group going back to the carpet square. Start the music, and have the children follow the leader around the room in any manner the leader chooses (hopping, crawling, skipping, and marching are a few possibilities). When the music stops, whoever is on the carpet square becomes the new Moses and everyone follows his or her lead.

Follow Me

Supplies: A large candle or a flashlight and a cloud cut from paper or a handful of cotton batting

Scripture: Exodus 13:17-22

Energy Level: Medium

Play this game after you have learned about Moses and the children of Israel following God in the pillars of cloud and fire.

Have the children stand in a straight line so that they all are facing the teacher. They should be standing so that if they wanted to follow the leader, they would have to take side steps to do it.

Say: **Who is the line leader in this line? It depends on which direction we go, doesn't it? In our story today, the children of Israel were led by God. Sometimes God appeared as a fiery pillar** (hand the candle or flashlight to the child on one end) **and sometimes he appeared as a pillar of cloud** (hand the cloud to the child on the other end). Say: **Today we are going to pretend that one line leader is the fiery pillar and the other line leader is the pillar of cloud.**

Say: **When I call out "Pillar of Fire!" turn to follow the person who is holding the candle. When I call out "Pillar of Cloud!" make an about-face and follow the person who is holding the cloud.**

Before beginning the game, have children practice making about-faces in their line. For younger children, be sure to stop the action for a moment before they follow the new leader. For older kids, switch more abruptly. Change leaders frequently.

Coach's Comment

This is great fun to play outside with older preschoolers, especially if there is play equipment for more creative following opportunities.

Me and My Manna

Supplies: Popped popcorn, a clean bedsheet or a piece of plastic sheeting, and enough small paper bags for each child to have one

Scripture: Exodus 16

Energy Level: Medium

Kids will become dramatic characters who find themselves transported to an ancient desert for this tempting, tasty treat.

Say: **Today we are going to find out what it was like for the Israelites to wander around in the sandy desert.** Have the children follow your lead as you take them through the desert. Say: **Drag your feet through the hot sand. Climb up that next tall dune. Oops! You went the wrong way! Turn around and go back. Imagine that you had been wandering for forty-five days and your tummy was growling. Start to grumble about how hungry you are as you keep walking and walking. Now stop grumbling because it's getting dark and you're too tired to even talk! Lay down with your eyes closed. Keep your eyes closed until I tell you it's morning.** Leave an area open so you can spread out the sheet or plastic with a layer of popcorn spread over it while the children have their eyes closed.

Say: **The Lord heard the grumbling of his people, and he sent a miracle in the morning. When the grumbly people woke up, there was "manna" scattered all over the ground. They gathered just enough to eat that day.** Give each of the children a bag. Have them each fill up a bag and then sit down to eat their "manna" snack.

Gimme Ten!

Supplies: A stack of index cards and several pillows

Scripture: Exodus 20

Energy Level: High

Children will climb the mountain and get the commandments to take back to the children of Israel.

Stack the pillows on one side of the play area. Have the children stand on the other side. Say: **In our Bible story, Moses left the children of Israel and climbed a mountain where God gave him two tablets with commandments written on them. Each of you will get a chance to climb the pillow mountain, and I will hand you two cards, like the tablets with the commandments written on them that God gave to Moses. All the children of Israel on the other side of the room will count the commandments with me. Then Moses will run back to the children of Israel and tap the next person to come and get some cards.**

Play until each child has had a turn. Then teach children the following chant:

1, 2, 3, 4, 5 *(tap the first card once for each number)*,

6, 7, 8, 9, 10. *(Tap the second card once for each number.)*

God gave these commandments

To all women and men!

Moses and the Meeting Tent

Supplies: A sheet, four chairs, and string or rubber bands

Scripture: Exodus 33:7-10

Energy Level: Medium

Preschoolers will become honorary Israelites in this game that recalls worship in the desert.

Build a tent by placing the sheet over the tops of the four chairs. Secure the sheet with the string or rubber bands. Have the children stand around the tent. Explain that when Moses went inside the tent, God spoke with him there, and the Israelites worshiped outside the tent.

Say: **I'm going to choose one child to be Moses. When Moses goes inside the tent, you'll all drop to your knees and raise your hands to show that you're worshiping God. When Moses comes out, stand up quickly. Moses will touch one of you on the shoulder, and that person gets to be the next Moses. The old Moses will stand in that person's place.**

When it's your turn to be Moses, you can run quickly through the tent, crawl slowly, or do whatever you want to do. It's our job to watch carefully so we know when you go into the tent or come out of the tent!

Play until everyone has had a turn.

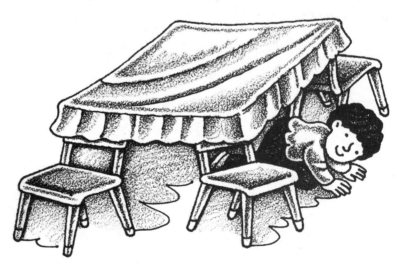

Moses, Miriam, and Aaron

Supplies: Small bags of M&M's candies, small bags of apple chips, and a disposable bowl for every three children

Scripture: Exodus

Energy Level: Medium

Use this snack/game combo with any story that mentions Moses, Miriam, and Aaron together.

Have the kids be seated in a circle, and tell them to close their eyes. Walk around the circle, and give each child a bag of candies or apples. Make sure that there are two times as many bags of candies as bags of apple chips. (If your class is not divisible by three, add or subtract the teacher or have a spare child pass out the snacks.) Say: **Each of you has a bag in your hands. When you open your eyes, look at your bag and then get together with two other friends so that your group has two bags that are the same and one bag that's different. When your group is together, freeze! When every group gets it right, we'll make a snack to share. If there's a group that doesn't get two bags the same and one different, I'll say "seek." Then you'll try to find some different friends who can help you make a group. Remember, you need two bags the same and one different. We'll work together until every group is right, just as Moses, Miriam, and Aaron worked together to help all the Israelites get it right!**

You may need to help the children get together in groups. As you check the groups, emphasize bags that are the same and different. Identify each child in a group as either Moses (candy), Miriam (candy), or Aaron (apple chips), and congratulate kids for working together. If the children need to regroup, encourage them to choose different partners. (You may want to regroup several times just for fun!) When all groups are correctly formed, give each "family group" a bowl and then let children mix the snack and enjoy it together.

The Israelites' Journey

Supplies: Masking tape

Scripture: Exodus

Energy Level: High

Use this game with stories about the Israelites wandering in the desert or possessing the land of Canaan.

Play this game in a large open area. Mark off a space with masking tape in the center of the area that is small enough so that the children in your group can encircle the area while holding hands.

Start the game by spacing the kids around the outer boundaries of your play area so that they won't bump into each other. Have them slowly spin their bodies as you sing this rhyme to the tune of "Ring Around the Rosie:"

Wandering outside the Promised Land,
The Israelites could not stand.
Griping, grumbling,
They all fall down. *(Children drop to the ground.)*

Repeat this until the children become familiar with the rhyme. Then have them hold hands around the center area you have marked off and march in place as you sing the next verse of the rhyme:

Closer to the Promised Land;
Hold each other by the hand—
Working together,
We all jump in! *(Children jump into the circle.)*

A Different Kind of Offering

Supplies: A bag of unsalted, popped popcorn; a saltshaker; melted butter in a squeeze bottle; small paper cups; a large bowl or pot; and napkins or paper towels

Scripture: Leviticus 2

Energy Level: Medium

Use this game when you teach about God's plan for giving.

Say: **The Israelites showed their obedience to God by following his directions about everything they did. God commanded them to bring him offerings, but they didn't have money to give him. Instead, he asked them to bring a part of what they owned. He gave them careful instructions about how they were to give their offerings. One kind of offering was a grain offering.**

We're going to use a grain that all of you know about—popcorn! Follow my directions carefully, just as the Israelites followed God's directions.

Have the children line up on one side of the room with the bag of popcorn at the front of the line. Place the bowl or pot, the squeeze bottle of butter, and the saltshaker at the other side of the room. Give each child a paper cup. Say: **You will take a cupful of popcorn and then get it to the bowl any way you choose. You may hop, skip, or just walk. Put the popcorn in the bowl and then squirt just a little butter on it, just as the Israelites poured oil on their offerings. Then sprinkle salt on top. To the Israelites, salt was a reminder of the promises they had made to God and God had made to them. Do these three things quickly so that you can come back to the line and the next person can go. When we're all finished, we will enjoy the offering as the priests at the temple did.**

When all the children have completed the game, mix up the contents of the bowl and enjoy the popcorn together. (You may want to have a backup supply, in case the "offering" is a little too salty!) Give children napkins or paper towels to wipe hands and faces.

Spies

Supplies: A bunch of plastic grapes (or real ones if you'd like to share them as a snack!)

Scripture: Numbers 13

Energy Level: Low

Kids will spy out the grapes of the Promised Land in this quiet game.

Designate an area large enough for all the children to sit in as home camp. Seat the children in another area, and show them the grapes.

Say: **Imagine our room is the Promised Land. You're all going to be spies, like Joshua and Caleb. You'll be looking for these grapes. When you find them with your eyes, go to the home-camp area and sit quietly. Don't tell anyone else where the grapes are!**

Have the children hide their eyes while you place the grapes somewhere in the room in plain sight.

Say: **You may open your eyes now and use them to spy out the grapes. When you have found the grapes, move over to home camp! Remember, don't tell where they are, just move quietly, like a spy.**

When all the children are seated in home camp, have them tell you where the grapes are. Play the game several times and then enjoy the grapes together.

Bible Heroes and Psalms

Down Come the Walls

Supplies: Old milk cartons, small boxes, or cardboard blocks; masking tape; several beach balls; and a horn or a whistle

Scripture: Joshua 6

Energy Level: High

Finish the story of the walls of Jericho with a rousing round of this game.

Line the milk cartons, boxes, or blocks up side by side and several rows high to form a wall. Mark a throwing line with masking tape several feet away from the wall. Have all the children stand behind the line. Select a child to be the horn blower, and give him or her the horn or whistle. Pass the beach balls to several children.

Say: **Remember how the walls of Jericho came falling down when Joshua gave the signal? Today we're going to use these balls to knock down the walls. In the Bible, God told Joshua to march around the city once a day for seven days before attacking, so we'll march in place and count to seven before our horn blower blows the horn. If you're holding a ball when you hear the horn, throw the ball at the wall. If you don't have a ball the first time, you'll have a turn soon.**

Play one round and then repair the wall and have different children hold the balls. Continue playing until everyone has had a turn to knock down the wall.

Ruth's Run

Supplies: Two large bowls, dry beans, and small paper cups

Scripture: Ruth 2

Energy Level: Medium

Preschoolers will get a feel for the hard work of Ruth in this fast-paced relay.

Fill one of the bowls with the beans, and place it on the floor. Place the empty bowl on a table across the room. Have the children stand in line near the bowl of beans. Say: **Let's carefully take turns as we move every bean from this bowl to the other one.** Let the children take turns stooping to fill their cups, walking across the room, and dumping the beans in the empty bowl. Say: **The Bible tells us about Ruth, who worked hard stooping to scoop up grain and carry it home so that she and her mother-in-law could eat.**

Let the children repeat the game as long as they show interest.

Samuel, Samuel

Supplies: A pillow

Scripture: 1 Samuel 3

Energy Level: Low

Illustrate the story of God talking to Samuel as he slept in the temple.

Make a circle. Pick one child to be Samuel. Say: **As Samuel was sleeping, he heard a voice calling his name. Our Samuel will lay down and pretend to go to sleep. Then I will point to one of you, and the person I point to will softly call, "Come here, Samuel."** Have the child playing Samuel lay down in the middle of the circle and pretend to go to sleep with his or her head on the pillow and his or her eyes closed. When the child closes his or her eyes, pick one child in the circle to say, "Come here, Samuel." Samuel will then "wake up," walk over to whoever he or she thinks was talking, and say, "I am here." If Samuel guesses correctly, the two children trade places. If the guess was incorrect, the person who called says, "Go back to bed." Then Samuel can try again. Play until everyone has had a chance to be Samuel.

Is This the One?

Supplies: None

Scripture: 1 Samuel 16:1-13

Energy Level: Low

Reenact the story of David's anointing as king of Israel.

Have the class stand. Choose one child to be Samuel.

Say: **The Bible tells us that Samuel went to the house of Jesse to choose one of Jesse's many sons to be king.** Today we are going to pretend that you are Jesse's children. Samuel is going to close his eyes, and I will point to a David so the rest of you will know who should be anointed king. Then Samuel will open his or her eyes. Samuel will go around to different children and ask, "Is this the one?" You will all answer, "No, that's not the one" or "Yes, that's the one."

When David has been guessed, he or she becomes the new Samuel. The retired Samuel becomes one of Jesse's sons. Continue the game until everyone has had a turn to be Samuel or David.

Small and Mighty

Supplies: A paper plate, old newspapers, masking tape, and trash bags or a trash can

Scripture: 1 Samuel 17

Energy Level: High

Kids will toss soft "stones" at a high target to get an idea of what David's battle with Goliath might have been like.

Mount the paper plate on a wall with tape. For younger kids, place it at eye level. For older preschoolers, mount it about nine feet high. Mark a line with masking tape for the kids to stand on. The distance from the wall will be determined by their skill level. Say: **Today we are going to see how hard David might have had to work to hit his target. Watch and I'll show you how.** Demonstrate how to wad up newspaper into stones to throw at the paper plate. Say: **Everyone will need to throw from behind this line so no one will get hit.** Demonstrate how to aim and throw the stones.

If you run out of paper, call a timeout and sweep all the stones to the children's side of the line. The children won't want to stop playing this game, but be sure you allow enough time for them to help you stuff the stones into trash bags or a trash can.

True Friends Stick Together

Supplies: A medium-sized lightweight ball or balloon for every two children and a basket or a large box

Scripture: 1 Samuel 20

Energy Level: Medium

Kids will stick closer than brothers as Jonathan and David in this fun partner game.

Assign each child a partner, naming one partner in each pair Jonathan and one partner David.

Have the partners in each pair stand back to back with a ball or balloon between them. They must walk the length of the room and drop the ball or balloon into the basket or box. If another pair is already at the box, the pair must stand and wait without dropping the balloon or ball. Children can switch partners if they want to continue playing.

Give partners in each pair high fives, and say: **You worked together just like Jonathan and David did. It sure is nice to have a friend to stick with.**

Younger preschoolers will be challenged by holding the balls with their partners using their hands. Older kids may want to try using elbows, wrists, tummies, or heads!

Hide in the Hills

Supplies: Two rows of chairs

Scripture: 1 Samuel 23:24-29

Energy Level: High

Saul's soldiers are foiled again in this game of "hide and hunt."

Set up two rows of chairs back-to-back, with the chair backs touching each other. To increase the area the children will travel around, increase the distance between the chairs as space allows. Choose half of the children to be David's soldiers and half to be Saul's soldiers. Line groups up on opposite sides of the chairs. Tell the children that the chairs are mountains. They may not go between the chairs but must stay in line moving around the chairs. Saul's soldiers are on one side of the mountains and David's are on the other side.

Saul's soldiers each need to shade their eyes with one hand as though they are looking for something, and David's soldiers need to keep looking over their shoulders. Position yourself between the two teams so that Saul's soldiers cannot move ahead of you.

Say: **Saul's soldiers are going to chase David's soldiers, but since everyone is carrying heavy equipment, no one can run—only walk fast. Be sure not to walk ahead of the person in front of you. David's soldiers, make sure you don't get too close to Saul's army or they will find you! I am the messenger. When I say, "The Philistines are attacking our land," Saul's soldiers must hurry back home. We'll say the wall is home. When all of Saul's soldiers have gotten to the wall, David's soldiers may be seated in the chairs to rest. Don't sit down until you are sure all of Saul's soldiers are all the way home!**

When Saul's soldiers have almost caught up with David's, say: **The Philistines are attacking our land!** Wait until all of Saul's soldiers are at the wall and David's soldiers are seated. Congratulate the groups for completing the game and then switch roles.

Abigail's Feast

Supplies: A serving tray, small pieces of bread, grapes, raisins, juice, and small paper cups

Scripture: 1 Samuel 25

Energy Level: Medium

Follow the story of Abigail and David with this game/snack combo.

Have one child stand near the serving tray and the other children stand on the other side of the room. Say: **Abigail took care of David and his friends by giving them food. One at a time, you will run across the room and** (child's name)**, our first Abigail, will give you something to eat or drink. After you have gotten your snack, you will become the new Abigail. The old Abigail will tap the next person in line and then go to the end of the line to wait for a snack.** For older preschoolers, Abigail can put the food in the children's mouths.

Saul and David's Hide-and-Seek

Supplies: A water pitcher and a broom

Scripture: 1 Samuel 26

Energy Level: Medium

Simple props bring this familiar game to life.

Say: **David had a chance to hurt Saul when he found him sleeping, but instead he chose to protect Saul. Who would like to pretend to be King Saul and hold this water jug and spear?** Hand the volunteer the pitcher and the broom. Say: **Saul will hide and pretend to be asleep, and the rest of us will try to find him.** Whisper to Saul that when the other children find him or her, he or she should let them take the jug and the spear. Take the children out of the room so that King Saul can hide. When a child finds King Saul, tell the finder to take Saul's sword and water jug. Then have all the children wake Saul up by saying, "Look what we have, Saul!"

Have Saul respond by saying, **"You took my sword but let me stay. Now it's** (child's name) **turn to play."** King Saul will choose a child to replace him or herself. Repeat the game several times.

Holy Ground

Supplies: None

Scripture: 1 Kings 6

Energy Level: Medium

Help preschoolers get to know their own church as you play this game based on Solomon's temple.

In this game, you will lead children through an imaginary visit to Solomon's temple. Say: **God told King Solomon to build a huge and wonderful temple. Each stone and piece of wood was put in its own special place. Everything was perfect in the temple Solomon built for God. Let's pretend that we are touching each part of this special temple Solomon built. Remember how special the temple was. You'll need to walk and touch each thing gently because each one is very special.**

Lead the kids through a series of items to touch in your classroom by saying things such as "touch something red," "touch something hard," and "touch a window." Continue by having the kids take turns naming items for others to touch. In an older group, encourage each child to touch a different object rather than touching the same thing someone else is touching. Make the game more challenging by having the kids each touch one item and keep touching it as they respond to the next instruction.

For more fun, schedule a time to lead the kids into your sanctuary or chapel. Encourage them to learn many of the parts of this holy place by having them reverently touch. "Pew," "altar," "stained-glass window," "cross," and "Bible" are just a few of the new words and phrases kids can learn about through touch.

Blackbird Express

Supplies: A bowl, napkins, and some fish-shaped crackers
Scripture: 1 Kings 17:1-6
Energy Level: Low

Kids can "fly" like ravens in this game to accompany the story of Elijah.

Seat children in a circle around a chair with an empty bowl under it. Choose one child to be Elijah, and have him or her sit in the chair. Give each of the seated children a napkin and a fish-shaped cracker. Tell them to wrap the crackers inside the napkins.

Say: **God told Elijah to go to a special place where he would send ravens to feed Elijah. Everyone in the circle is going to be a raven. While Elijah is sleeping with his or her eyes closed, I am going to tap one of you on the head. The one I tap is going to fly like a bird over to Elijah. That person will put the cracker into the bowl and then fly back to sit down. We will all say, "Elijah, Elijah, open your eyes and you will find a big surprise!" When we say that, Elijah's eyes will open. Then Elijah can guess which of you little birds brought dinner.** (Elijah may eat the cracker after he or she guesses.)

After three guesses, the person who fed Elijah becomes the new Elijah and the retired Elijah joins the circle. Continue playing until everyone has had a turn.

Elijah's Altar

Supplies: A ball

Scripture: 1 Kings 18:16-46

Energy Level: Medium

This circle game will help kids remember Elijah's soggy sacrifice to the living God.

Have the children sit in a circle on the floor and begin passing the ball around the circle. Say: **Listen while you pass the ball, and when you hear me say, "The Lord is God," I want the person holding the ball to throw it into the air. The ball will come down like the fire came down from heaven in our story. One person will catch the ball when it comes back down and then pass the ball to his or her neighbor. Everyone will get a turn to throw the ball in the air.** Have kids continue passing the ball around the circle, and give each of the children a chance to throw the ball into the air. Say: **Even though Elijah poured water on the sticks and the meat, God sent fire down from heaven and burned everything on the altar. God performed a miracle when Elijah prayed and asked him to show the people that God was the only true God.**

Rain, Rain, Ahab

Supplies: None

Scripture: 1 Kings 18:45-46

Energy Level: High

Children will enjoy playing this version of Duck, Duck, Goose after hearing the story of Elijah and the miracle of outrunning Ahab's chariot.

Have the children all sit in a circle facing the middle. Choose one child to be Elijah. Say: **Today we're going to play "Rain, Rain, Ahab." In the Bible, Elijah warned King Ahab that there was a big rainstorm coming. When Ahab got into his chariot, God helped Elijah outrun Ahab and his chariot all the way down a mountain. When you are Elijah, walk behind your friends and tap each one on the head and say "rain" until you get to someone who you want to chase you. Then tap that person's head and say "Ahab." Ahab will chase you as you run all the way back around the circle to the space that Ahab left open and sit down quickly. Ahab will be the new Elijah.** Add detail by showing the kids how to wiggle their fingers to make "raindrops" as they tap their friends. Allow each child to have a turn as Elijah, even if Ahab catches Elijah.

Sour Stew

Supplies: Several lemons cut in half, sugar, a wide-mouthed pitcher, a spoon, paper cups, and napkins

Scripture: 2 Kings 4:38-41

Energy Level: Low

Children will make a modern version of Elisha's gourd stew—phew!

Say: **Elisha told his friends to go squeeze some gourds and make a stew out of them. Let's make a drink by squeezing these lemons and see how the stew might have tasted to Elisha's friends.** Give each of the children a lemon half and a napkin, and have kids squeeze their lemon halves into the pitcher. Once all the lemon halves have been squeezed, add water to the pitcher but no sugar. Pour each of the children a very small sample. After the children have each had a sour taste, ask them what they think about their concoction.

Say: **Elisha heard his friends' complaints about their terrible tasting stew, too, so he added something to it to make it taste better.** Have each child come up and add a spoonful of sugar to the pitcher. Mix it well. Taste a bit yourself, and adjust the sugar if necessary.

Sing this song to the tune of "Row, Row, Row Your Boat" as the children add the sugar:

"We can't eat this stew!"
Elisha heard them say.
"Fix the stuff that's in this pot,
Or throw it all away!"

Say: **Let's taste our lemon stew now and see if it tastes better!** Let each child enjoy a glass of the new mixture.

Then have kids sing the second verse to the song:

"Yum! Yum! Yum!" they said. *(Rub your tummy.)*
"It tastes better now. *(Extend your arms upward.)*
God helped you to fix this stew.
Elisha, take a bow!" *(Bow from the waist.)*

Naaman's Dip

Supplies: An adult-sized white dress-shirt and a sheet

Scripture: 2 Kings 5:1-14

Energy Level: Medium

Children will love taking part in this game about Naaman's miraculous healing.

Say: **Naaman had a problem. He had a disease that made his skin look white. When he went to the prophet Elisha and asked to be healed, Elisha told him to go dip himself in the Jordan River seven times. Let's take turns pretending to be Naaman.** Have the first volunteer put the white dress-shirt over his or her clothes (it does not need to be buttoned). Have the rest of the children take hold of the sheet around the edges. Have the children lift the sheet in the air as high as they can and then wave it up and down like waves on a river. Tell Naaman to step under the "river" and dip up and down seven times while you all count to seven. Before Naaman comes out, have him or her take the shirt off. Rotate positions, and let each child have a chance to be Naaman.

Joash Rebuilds

Supplies: Plastic or wood construction blocks (about ten for each pair of children)

Scripture: 2 Kings 11:21–12:14

Energy Level: Low

After learning about Joash the boy king, older preschoolers will love working together to complete block "temples."

Assign each child a partner. Say: **The youngest king in the Bible was a seven-year-old boy named Joash. He made God happy because he told the people to rebuild God's temple. He had help from a wise friend whose name was Johoiada. Let's pretend that these blocks are parts of the temple, and you and your partner will work together to rebuild the temple.**

One person in each pair will be Joash. This person will be the builder. The other person will be Johoiada. This person will give Joash the blocks and directions about where to put them. Choose a child to be your helper so that you can model giving directions. This will help each Johoiada to get the idea of how he or she should give directions. Pick up one block, and say: **Stand this block up tall.** Give the child the block and then pick up another and say: **Put this block beside it.** Pick up another block, and say: **Put this one on top.** Keep giving directions until the temple is complete.

Distribute blocks to each pair of children (about ten per pair). Decide who will be Joash and who will be Johoiada in each pair. Allow the children to work on their own temples just as you have modeled. Have partners trade roles after they use all the blocks.

Block Building for Nehemiah

Supplies: Large lightweight blocks such as cardboard-brick blocks or small boxes and chalk or masking tape

Scripture: Nehemiah 4

Energy Level: Medium

Use this cooperative game along with the story of Nehemiah's great work-crew.

Say: The Bible tells us about a man named Nehemiah. He asked the Lord to help him and his friends build up a broken-down wall around the city of Jerusalem. Two men, Sanballat and Tobiah, tried to stop them from building the wall. But Nehemiah and his friends worked together with all their hearts and rebuilt the wall all around the city.

Teach the children the following rhyme. Have them clap their hands while they are reciting the rhyme.

The people worked with all their might;
They built with blocks both day and night.
Mean men came and tried to fight;
The wall was built in all men's sight.

Form two groups. Make a line with chalk or masking tape between the two groups, and set half the blocks on the floor behind each group. Tell children they are to work together to build the wall along the line like Nehemiah and his friends did. Help each group of children get into a line. Have the last child in line pick up a block and pass it down the line of children. The child closest to the wall places the block on the wall and then goes back to the stack of bricks to be the last person in line. Select two children to be Sanballat and Tobiah. Assign one to each group to distract the builders in some way without touching them or their blocks.

Tell the workers not to let Sanballat and Tobiah stop their work. Encourage the children to recite the poem aloud while they're building the wall. Periodically stop the game and allow different children to be Sanballat and Tobiah.

Allow the children to build, knock down, and rebuild the wall as long as they are having fun.

Crown the Queen

Supplies: A picture to represent Queen Esther, one flat paper crown that can be taped to the picture for each child, tape, and a dark-colored stocking cap

Scripture: Esther 2:1-18

Energy Level: Low

Preschoolers will help King Xerxes crown his new queen in this party game.

Mount the picture of Queen Esther on the wall. Make a circle of tape to go on each child's crown.

Say: **Today we'll play "Crown the Queen." When it's your turn, I'll pull the stocking cap down over your eyes. Then I'll give you a crown. We'll count to three while I spin you around. Then you'll walk up to the wall and stick the crown on Queen Esther's head. After everyone has had a turn, we'll see who came closest to crowning the queen.**

If you play this with two-year-olds, you can eliminate the stocking cap and the spinning. They'll think it's fun just to walk up and stick on the crown.

The King's Scepter

Supplies: A baton or a stick to use as a scepter

Scripture: Esther 5:1-7

Energy Level: Medium

Kids will watch the king's scepter carefully in this game that will help develop quick reactions.

Have the children form a line standing side by side facing a goal at the end of your playing area. Make sure the goal can be identified easily. For example, use a line of chairs or tables if you are inside or use a walkway or a fence for outside play.

Say: **When Queen Esther wanted to talk with the king, she had to wait until he held out his scepter to her. Let's pretend that we have a king and that we can't move until he holds out his scepter.**

Give one child the scepter to hold. If you have a crown, put it on his or her head. Place that child at the goal line. Point out the goal to all of the children, and explain that they are trying to reach the goal by walking forward while the king has his or her scepter out. Tell the king to raise and lower the scepter whenever he or she wants.

Say: **You must keep your eyes on the king all the time. When he holds his scepter out, you can walk. When he puts it down, you must freeze. If you move after the scepter is down, you'll go back and start over. If you run instead of walk, you'll start over. Whoever walks to the goal first will be the next king.**

Twenty-Third Psalm Slalom

Supplies: Classroom chairs, a stuffed lamb or a lamb puppet, a pillow, a dishpan of water, and a yummy snack

Scripture: Psalm 23

Energy Level: Medium

This simple obstacle course helps emphasize the meaning of the Shepherd Psalm.

Set the room up as though there is an imaginary line down the center. Designate a starting point at one end of the room. Place one chair about five feet from your starting point, as far to the right of the room as possible. Place the second chair about five feet from the first chair on the left, the third chair five feet from the second chair on the right, and the fourth chair five feet from the third chair on the left, so that you have a zigzag course. Place the lamb on the first chair, the pillow on the second chair, the dishpan on the third chair, and the snack on the last chair.

Have each child choose a partner, and have pairs line up at the starting point. Walk through the course as you explain it to the kids. Say: **Our special game today has several directions. Listen carefully, and I'll show you how to play. Walk with your partner to the first chair. We'll all say, "The Lord is my shepherd, I shall not be in want." You and your partner will say "Baa!" to us.**

Then walk to the next chair. We'll say, "He makes me lie down in green pastures." You and your partner will lie down with your heads on the pillow.

Walk to the next chair, and we'll say, "He leads me beside quiet waters." You can splash in the water.

Walk to the last chair, and we'll say, "You prepare a table before me." Then you can take a snack and sit down at the end of the course, but don't eat your snack yet.

We'll say, "Surely goodness and love will follow me." Then the next two people will start.

When everyone has finished the course, we'll all yell out together, "And I will dwell in the house of the Lord forever! Amen." That will be the prayer for our snack time and then we can eat our snacks together.

Four in the Fire

Supplies: A hoop large enough for four children to stand inside it and strips of red fabric

Scripture: Daniel 3

Energy Level: High

Kids will find the friend who will deliver them from the flames.

Tie strips of red fabric to the hoop.

Play this game in a well-defined space so that children are easily caught.

Choose three children to be Shadrach, Meshach, and Abednego. Have them step inside the hoop and hold the hoop at their waists so that the "flames" are all around them. Choose one child inside the hoop to be the tagger. The tagger doesn't need to hold on to the hoop. They must move together to help the tagger tag a fourth child with his or her hands. When the tagger tags someone, that child will climb inside the hoop. The children will immediately drop the hoop so that it falls around the legs of all four children.

Teach the children this chant:

Nebuchadnezzar threw in three,

But I count four! How can that be?

One, two, three, four!

Come on out,

Let's play some more!

Choose three other children, and repeat the game.

Lion Hunt

Supplies: None

Scripture: Daniel 6

Energy Level: Medium

Children will hunt dangerous lions in this make-believe adventure through King Darius' country.

Ask: **Do you want to go on a lion hunt?** Explain to the children that they are to repeat what you say and do. Allow time after each statement for the children to do the actions and make the sound effects.

Open the gate. *(Make a creaky sound.)*

Close the gate. *(Make a creaky sound.)*

Through the tall grass *(rub your hands together)*,

Through the squishy mud *(make "bear claws" with your hands, and say, "squish, squish");*

I see a river, but there's a wobbly bridge we can cross. *(Sway from side to side.)*

Oh, look! There's a brook. Let's jump over it. *(Make your hands "run and jump.")*

Splash…we'll have to swim. *(Make swimming motions.)*

Shake yourself off. *(Shake yourself off, and pretend to sit in the sun.)*

Do you see a lion yet? *(Pretend to be looking.)*

No!

Maybe we can see better from that tree. *(Pretend to climb a tree.)*

I see a cave. Maybe the lion is in it. Let's go see. *(Pretend to climb down from the tree.)*

Shh! *("Tiptoe" with your fingers.)*

I see one eye. I see two eyes. Do you want to go on a lion hunt? *(Use a very shaky voice.)*

No!

Reverse all of the items in the dialogue but move and speak very rapidly until you and the children are safely "home."

It Looks Fishy

Supplies: A white plastic dropcloth; red, yellow, blue, green, and black permanent markers; and a spinner with red, yellow, blue, green, and black spaces or a cube marked with those colors

Scripture: Jonah

Energy Level: Medium

Use this game frequently during gathering times after children know the story of Jonah.

Before class, make a game mat by drawing a large fish in the center of the plastic dropcloth. Draw little fish (about the same size as your children's feet) to completely surround the big fish, about four inches apart. Make the colors of the little fish in a random pattern.

Teach the children to play the game. Say: **When it's your turn, start by standing on the big fish. Then one of us will take a turn spinning the spinner** (or rolling the cube) **to tell you where you should put a foot. Then someone else will spin** (or roll) **to see where you should put your other foot. We'll do the same thing with your hands. Try to stay balanced as you put your hands and feet on different fish.**

Older preschoolers can play this game two or three at a time, each choosing different little fish to balance on.

Stories About Jesus' Life

Follow the Star

Supplies: A flashlight

Scripture: Matthew 2:1-10

Energy Level: Medium

Children will chase the Christmas star in this fun game that reminds kids about the journey of the wise men.

Have children form two groups, lined up in relay-style lines. Make more groups if you have more than ten children.

Say: **A long time ago, a bright star came out in the sky to tell everyone that Jesus had been born. Wise men followed this star to find the baby Jesus. Today we are going to play a game where we can follow a star. I am going to turn off the lights, and the first person in each line is going to try to follow the shining star and step on it. When you hear me say, "You found the shining star!" both players should run back to their teams and let the next people in line try to find a star.** Both children can touch the star at the same time. This doesn't have to be a race.

Shine the light around the room on the floor. Make it challenging enough so the children have to try to step on the light. Make sure you control the light so children do not run into each other. Play until everyone has had a turn.

Well Pleased

Supplies: A feather

Scripture: Matthew 3:13-17

Energy Level: Low

Kids affirm each other in this game based on Jesus' baptism.

Have children sit in a circle. Say: **When Jesus was baptized, the Holy Spirit came down and said that God was pleased with him.** Today we are going to tell some things that please us about our friends. I'll blow this feather. When it lands on someone, I'll tell one thing about that person that has made me happy. Then the person who the feather landed on will blow the feather to someone else and tell something that has made him or her happy about that person. We'll play until everyone has had the feather. You may need to prompt less verbal children.

This is a great game to end with a prayer. Pray that God will help all of us be the kind of people who please him.

Temptation Stations

Supplies: A loaf of bread, children's Bibles, paper crowns or robes, and blankets

Scripture: Matthew 4:1-11

Energy Level: Medium

Set up these activity stations to follow the story of Jesus' temptation in the wilderness.

Set up three separate areas in your classroom as temptation stations. Say: **Today we're going to learn more about the ways that Satan tempted Jesus in the desert. The first thing Satan tried to get Jesus to do was to change rocks into bread.** At the first station, place children's Bibles and a loaf of bread. Hold up the loaf of bread, and have kids sing this variation of "The B-I-B-L-E:"

**The B-R-E-A-D—
That's not enough for me.
It feeds my body, not my soul—
The B-R-E-A-D.**

Then have the children hold up the Bible and sing "The B-I-B-L-E."

Walk to the second area, and say: **The second thing Satan tried to get Jesus to do was to jump off a cliff and let angels catch him.** At the second station, lead the children in an imaginary mountain climb. When you arrive at the highest pinnacle, sing "Oh, Be Careful." When you get to the verse about feet, substitute this line: "Be careful, little feet, where you jump."

Walk to the third area, and say: **The third thing Satan tried to get Jesus to do was to worship Satan, not God.** At the third station, have the children try on robes or paper crowns and sit in mock thrones made by throwing blankets over classroom chairs. Have the children sing this song to the tune of "Row, Row, Row Your Boat:"

**No, no, no, I say!
You just go away!
I will worship God alone
And only him obey.**

Calm the Storm

Supplies: A sheet and lots of small balls or inflated balloons

Scripture: Matthew 8:23-27

Energy Level: High

Kids will create a storm as a backdrop for this high-energy game.

Say: One time Jesus was out in a boat with his friends, and a great storm came up that really scared everyone. Jesus calmed the storm because he didn't want his friends to be scared. Whenever you hear me say, "calm the storm" during this game, freeze in place.

Let everyone hold part of the outer edge of the sheet. Show the children how they can make gentle waves with the sheet. Then let them shake more strongly and make huge waves. Now add balls or balloons, and see if the children can bounce them out. When they get used to this, form two teams. One team holds the sheet and bounces the balloons or balls out in the wild storm while the other team throws the balloons back onto the sheet. After a few minutes, say: **Calm the storm.** Everyone will freeze in place. Then have the teams trade positions.

Caring Carriers

Supplies: One towel for every four students and one inflated balloon with a face drawn on it for every four students

Scripture: Matthew 9:1-8

Energy Level: High

Kids will carry balloon "friends" in this cooperative game that goes along with the story of Jesus healing the paralytic.

Help children gather in groups of four at one end of the play area. Give each group a towel and direct the children to each hold a different corner of the towel. Introduce them to their new balloon friend, who can't walk by himself. Place a balloon on each towel. The teacher or one of the children will pretend to be Jesus at the other end of the play area. When you call out "go!" the children will carry their balloon friends to the other side of the room. The challenge will be to keep the balloons from falling to the ground. Praise each group as it accomplishes its goal.

Gather in new groups of four and play again.

Shriveled Hands

Supplies: Chalk and a chalkboard or markers and two large sheets of paper and a sock for each team

Scripture: Matthew 12:9-14

Energy Level: Low

Help kids get a feel for the story of the healing of the man with the shriveled hand as they play this creative game.

Make at least two teams. Have teams stand in relay-style lines facing the chalkboard or two large sheets of paper attached to a wall. Make a circle on each drawing surface to be the man's head. Draw a frown on his face. Tell the kids that they are going to fill in the man's face one part at a time, but they have to wear the sock on their drawing hands. The first person in each line puts the sock on and runs to draw a feature on the face. When he or she is finished, he or she takes the sock off and gives it to the next person in line. When everyone has had a turn, say: **It was hard for the man to do anything with his shriveled hand. That must have made him sad. But Jesus told him to stretch out his hand, and it was healed. That made him happy.** Draw another circle on each sheet of paper or each side of the chalkboard, this time with smiles instead of frowns.

Play again without the socks. Say: **After Jesus healed the man's hand, it was easy for the man to use it, just as it was easier for you to use your hand without the sock over it!**

Baskets Full of Smiles

Supplies: None

Scripture: Matthew 14:13-21

Energy Level: Low

never run out of fun in this game to accompany the feeding of the five thousand.

Have two teams line up in relay-style lines.

Say: **Only one little boy brought fish and bread to lunch, but when he shared, Jesus used the food to feed the whole crowd. Everyone was happy. We're going to see if you have a happy face you can share, because Jesus can use your shared smile to make others happy.**

Instruct the first person in each line to make a happy, silly face and show it to the person behind him or her. That person imitates the face and shows it to the person behind him or her until the face has gotten all the way to the end of the line. The person at the end of the line runs up to the beginning of the line and makes a different face. Play continues until everyone has had a turn.

Say: **You shared a happy, silly face with everyone until we all laughed. Looks like we have plenty of fun to go around and some left over, too!**

One Step at a Time

Supplies: A sheet

Scripture: Matthew 14:22-36

Energy Level: Medium

A sheet becomes the wind and the waves in this game based on Peter's water walk.

Form two teams. Have the teams kneel on the floor facing each other, about five feet apart.

Say: **Today we learned about Jesus and Peter walking on the water. The wind and the waves could have knocked Peter down into the water, and he would have drowned. Peter had to keep his eyes on Jesus to walk on the water.** Have the lines of children hold the sheet between them. Show them how to shake the sheet to make waves. Say: **Peter is going to try to walk through to the other side while the wind and the waves roll all around him or her. I'll be Jesus standing on the other side. Peter, don't look down. Just keep your eyes on me.**

Choose someone to be Peter, and have the rest of the children stay in their lines. Have kids continue shaking the sheet until Peter reaches the end of the line. Then have Peter sit down at the end of one of the lines, and have the child at the beginning of that line take his or her turn as Peter. Continue until everyone has had a turn.

Jesus Plays With the Children

Supplies: None

Scripture: Matthew 19:13-15

Energy Level: Medium

This game will help children know how much Jesus loved little children.

Say: One day Jesus had many little children come to him. Some of the older people, called disciples, didn't like the little children getting so close, but Jesus loved the little children.

Get the children into a circle with one person acting as Jesus in the middle. Use more than one circle if you have more than six preschoolers. Have them hold hands and stretch their circle out until their arms are extended.

Have the children walk in a circle around Jesus as they sing this song to the tune of "Have You Ever Seen a Lassie?":

Have you ever seen Jesus,
Seen Jesus, seen Jesus;
Have you ever seen Jesus
Turn children away?
He loves us *(walk in close to Jesus),*
We love him *(take backward steps to enlarge the circle),*
He loves us *(walk in close to Jesus),*
We love him. *(Take backward steps to enlarge the circle.)*
Have you ever seen Jesus *(walk in a circle around Jesus again)*
Turn children away?

When children come into the center of the circle, they can gently give Jesus a hug. Let Jesus pick another child to be in the center to continue play.

Jesus Is Risen

Supplies: A table tipped over on its side in the room or in a closet

Scripture: Matthew 28:1-10

Energy Level: Low

Children will experience Jesus' resurrection as they meet the angel at the tomb.

Have the children sit on the floor facing a table tipped over on its side.

Say: **A long time ago, people were very sad because Jesus had died on the cross. Many closed their eyes and cried and cried.**

Explain to the children that you will pick one child to hide behind the table and pretend to be the angel who told people about Jesus' resurrection.

Instruct children to pretend to cry while covering their eyes. Then choose one child to secretly go hide behind the table. As the children open their eyes, the person behind the table will say, "He is risen." Let the children guess which child is pretending to be the angel. If a child guesses correctly, have the angel come out from behind the table and have all the children say, "He is risen."

Keep repeating the game until everyone has had a chance to hide. You might make it tricky and ask older children to try to make different voices when they are the angel.

Come Along

Supplies: None

Scripture: Mark 1:14-20

Energy Level: Medium

Reinforce the story of how Jesus chose his disciples by playing this choosing game.

Say: Remember how Jesus went along the Sea of Galilee asking people to become his disciples? Today we're going to pretend that we are being chosen, too. Help the children form a circle. Have them stand as if they were marching in a circle. Have each child put his or her outside hand out. Choose one child to be Jesus. Say: **When you are Jesus, walk around the circle and choose someone by taking his or her hand. That child will walk with you and catch the hand of someone else. We'll keep on choosing people until everyone has been chosen. Then we'll have a new circle, and we'll pick a new Jesus to start the next game.**

Coach's Comment

A word of warning when you're playing this game with older children: you may have to warn them not to move so rapidly that someone gets pulled to the ground.

Hear and Follow

Supplies: A scarf or another piece of fabric to use as a blindfold

Scripture: Mark 10:46-52

Energy Level: Medium

This game is a great accompaniment to the story of blind Bartimaeus.

Have the children form a circle. Choose one child to be blind Bartimaeus.

Say: **Today we learned about blind Bartimaeus and how Jesus healed him. Now we are going to play a game in which each of you will have a turn to be Bartimaeus. While Bartimaeus is blindfolded in the middle of the circle, I will point to someone to be Jesus.**

The circle will rotate and the person playing Jesus will say, "I will heal you." Bartimaeus will listen closely to the voice and try to find Jesus and gently touch him.

Stand in the center of the circle with Bartimaeus, and blindfold him or her. Have the circle slowly rotate. Twist Bartimaeus around three times and quietly point to someone in the circle to be Jesus. Jesus should start saying, "I will heal you," and continue saying it until he or she is identified. Let go of Bartimaeus so that he or she can follow Jesus' voice. Once Jesus is found, he or she will remove Bartimaeus' blindfold and trade places with Bartimaeus so the game can continue. Play until everyone has had a turn.

Prayer Bridge

Supplies: None

Scripture: Mark 14:32-42

Energy Level: Medium

Play this game to encourage prayer after the story of Jesus' prayer in the Garden of Gethsemane.

Have the children form a line. Choose a child to help you form a bridge.

Say: **In this story Jesus prayed for himself and for others. I want you to think of some things you can pray for as we begin to march under the bridge.**

Sing this song to the tune of "London Bridge":

God will listen when you pray,
When you pray, when you pray.
God will listen when you pray.
What will you say?

Drop the bridge, and capture a child. Ask the child to name something or someone you can pray about together. Say a sentence prayer with the child and then raise the bridge and start the song over again. Continue until everyone has a chance to be captured and to pray.

No, Not Me!

Supplies: A plastic egg filled with small candies such as jelly beans

Scripture: Mark 14:66-72

Energy Level: Low

Remember the story of Peter's denial in this sweet circle-game.

Have the kids sit closely together on the floor in a circle. Have one child stand in the middle of the circle to begin the game.

Say: **In this Bible story, Peter told people he was not one of Jesus' friends because he was afraid. When Peter heard the rooster crow, he remembered that Jesus had said he would deny him. Let's pass this egg around behind our backs to remind us of chickens and roosters. Peter will stand in the center with his eyes closed. When Peter opens his eyes, he will try to guess who has the egg. If he guesses that you have it and you don't, say, "No, not me!" If you do have the egg, gently open the egg and take a piece of the candy. You can be the next Peter in the center.** Peter can keep guessing until he finds the right person. Then pass the egg again.

Play this game as long as children are interested. Be sure to pass the egg around the circle so that children who did not get a piece of candy can have one.

name Stomp

Supplies: None

Scripture: Luke 1:26-38

Energy Level: Low

Help kids stomp out the sounds of some special names after telling about how Jesus got his name.

Have the kids scatter around the middle of the room.

Say: **In this Bible story, the angel told Mary what the name of her special son would be. It was Jesus.** Show the kids how to stomp on each part of Jesus' name. **Your name was chosen especially for you, too. Let's take turns saying our first names out loud. We'll all stomp with our feet one time for each part of each person's name.**

Encourage the kids to stomp once for each part in the first name. Have them try doing the same thing with their last names. Or if they know their first, middle, and last names, have them stomp out those parts. When older kids have mastered this, have them each figure out whose name has the same pattern of stomps as their name does. Have children with the same pattern stand and stomp out the parts together. As you are nearing the end of the game, have the children stomp the phrase "Jesus loves me!" all together.

Coach's Comment

This activity is also a fun way to learn a short Bible verse or the point of a Bible lesson. Have the kids say the verse or lesson point while stomping out the syllables.

Missing in Action

Supplies: None

Scripture: Luke 2:41-52

Energy Level: Medium

Kids figure out who's missing in this Hide-and-Seek game.

Say: **In our Bible story, Jesus' family was walking home and suddenly noticed he was missing. In our game today, I'm going to count to twenty and let all of you hide. Then I'll find some of you and together, we will try to figure out who's still missing.**

Close your eyes and count slowly enough to allow all the children to hide. After you have found most of the kids, have them look around to see who is missing and call that person to come out. For more rounds, enlist a child to be the seeker after you count together.

Cast Your net

Supplies: A beach towel
Scripture: Luke 5:1-11
Energy Level: Medium

Kids will enjoy fishing for their friends in this game.

Have all the children stand in a circle. Choose two children standing together to be the fishers. Leave their spaces open. If you have a large group, make the opening about one-quarter of your circle. Have the fishers stand in the middle and hold the beach towel on both ends and practice swinging it up and over their heads. You may need to help them.

Chant the following rhyme as the children march to the left without closing the circle.

Fished all night and what did we get?
Not one fish in this great big net!

Have the fishers swing the net into the empty space. Then chant the next verse as children march to the right.

Here comes Jesus on the shore.
He says, "On the other side, you'll catch more!"

Have the fishers swing the net the other way over two children standing in the circle. These children will become the new fishers. Continue until everyone has had a chance to be a fisher.

Older children will enjoy swinging the net with their eyes closed and taking their chances on catching some fishy friends.

Dinner With Mary and Martha

Supplies: None

Scripture: Luke 10:38-42

Energy Level: High

Preschoolers will get better acquainted with Mary and Martha in this make-believe visit to their home.

Place half the children on one side of the play area and half on the other side. Line kids up side to side. Identify every other child on each team as either Mary or Martha.

To begin, give the children directions about how to move with the following chants:

Mary, Mary, full of peace,
Skip to the other side, if you please.
   or
Martha, Martha, full of care,
Hop to the other side, over there.

Marys and Marthas on each team will move to the opposite side of the room and take the places of those who left the other team's line. Alternate the chants, or give them in random order to challenge listening skills. Change the action word so that children move from side to side in different ways. When the kids all know the chants, have different children take turns giving the directions.

Coach's Comment

To help kids remember whether they are Marys or Marthas, draw worried faces for the Marthas and happy faces for the Marys on small pieces of masking tape and put one piece on each child's hand.

Spot, Spot...
Thanks a Lot!

Supplies: Small circular stickers

Scripture: Luke 17:11-19

Energy Level: Low

Emphasize the importance of a grateful heart with this fun game based of the healing of the ten lepers.

Say: **We're going to play a game with spots that will teach us to remember to say thank you, like the one leper who thanked Jesus for healing him.**

Place two or three circular stickers on the back of each child's hands or lower arms. Remind them that the spots are a disease that they don't want to have. Tell them you are going to take their spots away. If a child says, "Thank you" when you take a spot off, you will clap and cheer. If the child forgets to say, "Thank you," you will look very sad. Teach the children the following cheer to congratulate each classmate who gets rid of a spot:

Hooray, Hooray!

(Child's name) **remembered to be thankful today!**

Zacchaeus, Come Down

Supplies: A chair or a stool and photocopies of enough small hand-drawn tree-pictures to give one to each student. Color one tree, and leave the rest uncolored.

Scripture: Luke 19:1-10

Energy Level: Medium

Take this game about Zacchaeus outdoors for extra fun.

Say: **Jesus was walking through a town one day when he noticed a man sitting up in a tree. The man's name was Zacchaeus, and because he was short, he had climbed into the tree to see Jesus. Jesus called out to him, "Zacchaeus, hurry and come down! I must stay at your house today."**

Have the children form a circle. Set a chair or a stool in the middle of the circle. Hand out the tree pictures. The child holding the colored tree gets to be Zacchaeus and sit on the chair in the middle.

Say: **We're going to hold hands and move around in a circle.** Teach the children this song to the tune of "Are You Sleeping?":

Zacchaeus, Zacchaeus,
Please come down, please come down.
Jesus wants to see you, Jesus wants to see you.
Please come down, please come down.

Have Zacchaeus "come down" from the stool and select another child to sit in the center. Repeat the game until all the children have had the opportunity to be Zacchaeus. If you have an outdoor playground available to you, have Zacchaeus climb to the top of the slide or the jungle gym. The class can circle around the play equipment, but be sure to carefully supervise for safety.

At the Pool

Supplies: A child's wading pool or a dishpan and a two-liter bottle filled with small treats

Scripture: John 5:1-18

Energy Level: High

Play this fun game outdoors when you teach about the healing of the lame man at the pool of Bethesda.

Fill the wading pool or dishpan with water. Have the children stand an equal distance from the pool. Say: **In this Bible story, people who couldn't walk wanted to get to the water as soon as it started swirling. When you see me swirl the water in the pool with the bottle, get to the pool as quickly as you can without walking. You can crawl, wriggle, roll, or scoot; but you can't stand on your feet. When you get to the pool, put one hand in the water and hold the other hand up to me.**

Swirl the pool water with the bottle. When all the children have gotten to the pool, pour one of the treats from the bottle into each child's hand. Ask: **Which hand got the treat, the one in the water or the one reaching out to Jesus? It was Jesus who healed the man, not the water in the pool.** Play the game several times, encouraging the children to use different movements to get to the pool each time.

Donkey Colt

Supplies: A towel or a small blanket

Scripture: John 12:12-19

Energy Level: High

Children find a donkey colt and bring it back for Jesus in this playful game.

Have the children stand in two equal lines on each side of the play area. One side will be the donkeys, and the other side will be the disciples.

Hand the towel or blanket to the first disciple. Say: **Disciples, it is your job to go find a donkey for Jesus to ride into Jerusalem. Take the towel, and go get a donkey from the other side. Donkeys, you will get down on your knees. Let the disciple put the towel over your back and then both of you will go back to the other side together. Disciples, when you've finished, hand the towel to the next disciple, who will go to get another donkey colt.** Continue play until all the donkeys are on the disciples' side.

Switch roles and let the children play again if they are still interested.

neat Feet

Supplies: Enough baby wipes for each child to have one
Scripture: John 13:1-17
Energy Level: Medium

Children will serve each other as Jesus served his disciples at the Last Supper.

Have the children form a circle and be seated with their feet in front of them. Place the container of baby wipes in the center of the circle. Choose one child to be the first foot-washer.

Say: **Jesus served his disciples by washing their feet. Today we're going to wipe each other's shoes to help us remember that Jesus wants us to serve each other, too.**

Teach the children the following rhyme:

One foot, two feet,
Inside-your-shoes feet,
(Foot washer's name) **wants to serve you,**
As Jesus showed us how.

Have the foot washer walk around behind the children and stop on the word "how." Then have the foot washer and the child he or she stopped behind go to the center of the circle. Have the foot washer take a baby wipe and wipe the shoes of the second child. The foot washer will then take the place of the child he or she has served, and the child who has been served will be the new foot washer. (NOTE: the first foot washer will return to the circle with his or her feet still dirty.) When the second child returns to the circle, have him or her sit cross-legged to show the others that his or her feet have already been washed. If the new foot washer stops behind a child who is sitting cross-legged, he or she should proceed to the next child who still has his or her legs extended.

Stories Jesus Told

Lights and Bushels

Supplies: None

Scripture: Matthew 5:14-16

Energy Level: Medium

Preschoolers will love to let their lights shine in this fast-moving game.

This game is a simplified version of Rock, Paper, Scissors. Show the children how to make fists and pound them down on their palms twice. On the third pound, kids will need to choose whether to keep their fists closed like bushels or to hold up their index fingers like candles.

Have all the children go to one side of the play area. Stand at the end of the opposite side. On your signal, everyone will do the actions. You can count "one...two..." and on three everyone will show either a bushel or a candle. If a child's symbol matches the symbol you show, he or she takes a step forward. Play until everyone reaches you.

A fun way to make the point that we should always let our lights shine before men is to always give the candle symbol. Older preschoolers will soon catch on that the best way to succeed is to always give the candle symbol, too.

Shifting Sands

Supplies: Plastic or wood construction blocks, a blanket, and a piece of cardboard

Scripture: Matthew 7:24-27

Energy Level: Medium

Demonstrate the importance of building on a firm foundation with this block-building game.

Say: **Let's work together in two groups to build a house as big as we can. Half of you will build on this blanket, and the other half of you will build on the piece of cardboard.** After the groups have had some time to build houses, tell them about the second half of the game. Say: **Now I want each of your groups to carefully slide the blanket or the sheet of cardboard and work together to move your house across the room.**

Ask: **What happened? Did both groups build well? What was the difference?** Say: **That's the difference Jesus was telling people about when he talked about the man who built his house on the rock in our Bible story. People who build their lives on Jesus can stand firm, even when something comes along to shake them.**

Four Corners

Supplies: Balloons (one for every four children)
Scripture: Matthew 13:1-9
Energy Level: High

Challenge your preschoolers in this game based on the parable of the sower.

Make groups of four. Have each group make a small circle, and assign one of the following roles to each of the four children in each group:

● **Birds** put their hands at their ribs and flap their arms like bird wings. They can only use their "wings" to bat the balloon.

● **Rocks** put their hands at their sides and stand very still. They can only use their heads or shoulders to bat the balloon.

● **Thorns** put their hands at their sides. They can only use their legs and feet to kick the balloon.

● **Good dirt** stands relaxed. They can use either their hands or their feet to bat the balloon.

Say: **Today we are going to see how well you can pass the balloon around your group. You can only hit the balloon in the way I showed you, no matter what other people in your group are doing. Let's see how many times you can pass the balloon around your group.** Let the children trade roles and try this activity in each of the four roles. Ask: **What was the easiest way to play our game today?** Say: **When seeds fall on good soil, they grow quickly and easily. Our hearts are like good soil when we hear and do what God tells us to through the Bible, our church, and our parents.**

This game can be simplified for younger children by showing them one action at a time and having all the children perform the same action together.

Small Becomes Large

Supplies: A chalkboard and chalk or two large pieces of paper attached to the wall and markers or crayons

Scripture: Matthew 13:31-32

Energy Level: Medium

Kids will see how little things add up in this game based on the parable of the mustard seed.

Make two teams. Have the children in each team stand in a line facing the chalkboard or one of the large pieces of paper. Show the children how to draw a small dot at the bottom of the paper and then a dot on top of the first dot. The children will continue to add dots one at a time, each running back to tag the next person on his or her team after placing a dot. The game continues until each team creates the tallest dot-tower it can.

Say: **Your teams sure made tall towers! How did your tiny dots make such big, tall rows? Jesus told us about tiny mustard seeds turning into something big, just as our tiny dots did. Jesus also told us that if we had tiny mustard-seed faith, God could turn it into something really big.**

Hidden Pearls

Supplies: Jelly beans

Scripture: Matthew 13:44-46

Energy Level: Medium

Secrets abound in this hunt for hidden treasures.

Before playing this game, hide an abundance of jelly beans around the room. Reserve some extras in case you need them.

Gather the children together. Say: **There are special hidden treasures all over our classroom. They are small, like pearls. Here are some extra hints: they are brightly colored, and they taste good. In a minute, you are going to look for them. When you find one, don't pick it up. Leave it and come back here.**

When all the children have found treasures and have come back to you, teach them this chant:

The best pearl
In all the world
Is loving Jesus.

Have the children each go get a treasure and eat it. Then play the game again several times. Each time the children come back, change the second word in the last line of the chant to one of the following: "knowing," "serving," "helping," and "following." In the last rounds, you may need to help the children "find" jelly beans from your reserve.

Fishing Tax

Supplies: Lots of sheets of paper from a recycling bin, a few pennies, and a jump-rope

Scripture: Matthew 17:24-27

Energy Level: Medium

Preschoolers will seek coins from the mouths of fish in this fun fishing game.

Crumple the sheets of paper into balls to be "fish" for the game. Put pennies in a few of them, and wad them tightly enough to secure the money. Scatter all the fish in one general area in your room, but don't scatter them too close together.

Say: **Today we're going to look for money in the mouths of our pretend fish, but instead of using it to pay taxes, we'll collect it for our offering.**

Choose two children to be the fishers. Have one hold each end of the rope. These two will need to work together to use the rope as a net to gather in some of the fish. Once the fish are gathered, the rest of the children can begin opening the "caught fish" to see if they find a surprise. When a child finds a coin, have him or her place the money in a designated spot. Choose two new fishers, and continue playing until all the fish have been caught.

The Good Shepherd

Supplies: None

Scripture: Matthew 18:12-14

Energy Level: Low

This game correlates well with the parable of the lost sheep, and it could also be used with the many other biblical mentions of the Lord as a shepherd.

Have the children sit in a circle on the floor. Choose one player to be "It." Walk through the first round with the children to model the game.

The person who is "It" walks around outside the circle, stops behind one of the players, and asks, "Have you seen my sheep?" "What does your sheep look like?" asks the second child. The child who is "It" tells about another player in the circle by giving clues such as: "He is a boy" and "He is wearing shorts and a yellow shirt." The child in front of the person who is "It" looks around the group and guesses who the sheep is.

Continue the game, letting the child who guessed correctly be "It" next.

Workers in the Vineyard

Supplies: Treats

Scripture: Matthew 20:1-16

Energy Level: Medium

Equal rewards help children to understand the parable of the workers in the vineyard.

Have the children be seated in a circle. Call your circle the vineyard. Show the kids how to stoop over and pick grapes from an imaginary grapevine. Choose one child to be the landowner. The landowner will walk around the outside of the circle tapping one child to be a worker each time he goes around. As soon as they are tapped by the landowner, the children will stand and begin working in the vineyard, just as you showed them how to do.

As the game progresses, encourage all the children to "keep working" because you will give each of them a treat at the end of the game. Finally, when all the children have been tapped, tell them they may all be seated. Ask: **Who do you think is the most tired? Least tired?** Give them all the same treat.

Say: **The lesson Jesus was teaching in this story is that we all get the same reward for answering and obeying God. We don't need to worry if it looks like someone is doing more or less than we are. We just need to answer God when he calls.**

Children will enjoy playing this game again, even without rewards.

Ready or not

Supplies: Two identical flashlights, one with batteries and one with the batteries removed. Hide the batteries somewhere in the room.

Scripture: Matthew 25:1-13

Energy Level: Low

Remember the story of the wise and foolish virgins in this guessing game.

Show the kids how one flashlight works because someone was wise and put batteries in it. Show them how the other one won't work because it has no batteries. Even though the flashlights look exactly alike, one is ready to use and the other isn't.

Say: **You are going to be the people from our Bible story today. When I tell you to, you're going to get so sleepy that you have to lay down and pretend to be asleep. Keep your eyes shut. When I say, "The bridegroom is coming!" you'll each get up and stand by the flashlight you think will work. Then we'll see if you are ready or not!**

Coach's Comment

If you don't have identical flashlights, put the two flashlights in identical paper bags.

Move the flashlights randomly each time so that the kids have to guess. In each round, have all the children count the number of kids who are ready. After several rounds, say: **The people in our story weren't just guessing about who would be ready and who wouldn't be ready. Each of the people made a choice. What would the foolish ones need to do to get ready to shine their lights for the bridegroom? If you'd like to choose to get ready, you can search for batteries for the other flashlight. They are hidden somewhere in the room.** Give the children a chance to find the batteries and insert them into the second flashlight. Congratulate the children on choosing to be ready.

Watch It Grow

Supplies: Lots of small items, such as blocks

Scripture: Matthew 25:14-30

Energy Level: Medium

Kids put in what they are given in this cooperative game that connects to the parable of the talents.

Give each child two, three, or four small items. Ask if their piles are little or big. Say: **Your job is to use your pile, whether it is big or little, to make something even bigger!** Have the children stand in a line, each holding his or her items. Have the first child choose a way to get to the other side of the room, such as skipping, walking, or crawling, while still carrying his or her items. When the first child gets to the other side, he or she is to stack his or her items and walk back as fast as he or she can to touch the next person in line. The next person does the same thing. Teach kids this song to the tune of "If You're Happy and You Know It" to sing while everyone is completing the task:

If you've got a gift to use, bring it in.
If you've got a gift to use, bring it in.
If you've got a gift to use,
Let us share the happy news.
If you've got a gift to use, bring it in.

Say: **How does our collection look now? When we use what we have been given, we can make something much bigger than what we started with. It pleases God when we use the gifts he gives us.**

Helper or Holdout

Supplies: Adhesive bandages (with the outer wrapping removed), similar-sized rectangles of construction paper, a large stuffed animal or doll, and a brown-paper bag

Scripture: Luke 10:30-37

Energy Level: Low

Children will be helpers in this game based on the story of the Good Samaritan.

Place the bandages and the construction paper rectangles in the brown-paper bag, and shake it to distribute the items evenly. Place the large doll or stuffed animal in the middle of your play area.

Gather the children on one side of the play area. Say: **This animal will be the hurt man from our Bible story. I'll come around with this bag, and you'll each get a chance to reach in and take something out. If you take out a piece of paper, you'll just walk by our hurt man so that you can get to the other side of the room quickly. If you pull out a bandage, you'll stop and put it on our hurt man before you continue to the other side of the room, just as the Samaritan stopped to help the man in our story.**

Let the kids each select an item from the bag one at a time and walk to the other side. Play the game several times. Make sure that every child has had at least one bandage to place. If a child hasn't placed a bandage, make sure to give him or her one. Ask: **Did you think it was better to put the bandage on or to just walk by?** Say: **I'm proud of each of you for taking the time to be a helper.**

Find My Sheep

Supplies: None

Scripture: Luke 15:1-7

Energy Level: Low

Children will seek for lost sheep in this game that builds language and observation skills.

Have the children stand in a circle.

Say: **Jesus is the Good Shepherd who knows each one of his sheep. When one is lost, he goes and finds it. I am going to pretend to be a shepherd, but I need someone to help me find my sheep.**

Choose a child to stand with you in the center of the circle.

Say: **I am going to describe my lost sheep to you. As soon as you think you know who it is, go and get the sheep and bring it to me.**

Begin describing one of the other children. State the "sheep's" hair color, describe his or her clothes, and name any other distinctive characteristics. When your helper has correctly identified the child you were describing, direct the helper to stand in the circle and allow the sheep to be your new helper. Continue until all the children have been "found."

The Lost Coin

Supplies: A quarter and a music source

Scripture: Luke 15:8-10

Energy Level: Low

Transition games like this one make lining up a blast!

Have the children sit in a circle.

Say: **The woman who lost her coin was so excited when she found it that she went to tell her friends. In today's game, we are going to pass this coin around the circle while I play some music. When the music stops, whoever has the coin becomes the excited person who found it. That person leaves the circle to** (line up, choose an activity, or another option of your choice). **We will play until everyone has had a turn.**

Give one child the coin, and start the music. Play the game until everyone has lined up or chosen an activity.

Coach's Comment

Consider changing the prop in this game to make it fit with other stories. For example, you might use a star for a lesson on the wise men or a lamb puppet when you tell the story of the lost sheep.

The Youngest Son

Supplies: None

Scripture: Luke 15:11-32

Energy Level: Medium

Use this game with the story of the Prodigal Son.

Choose a child to be the father and one to be the elder son. They will stand with their hands raised and their fingertips touching. Have all the other children walk under the "bridge." Sing this song to the tune of "London Bridge:"

> The youngest son went far from home,
> Far from home, far from home.
> The youngest son went far from home
> And spent all his money. *(Have the father and the son drop their arms around the child who is passing under them at this point in the song.)*
> But his father loved him so *(have the father and the son hug the child between them)*,
> Loved him so, loved him so,
> But his father loved him so,
> He welcomed him home. *(Have the father and the son release the child.)*
> Repeat the game, choosing a new father and a new son.

The Early Church

Jerusalem, Judea, and Samaria

Supplies: A Bible for each child and masking tape

Scripture: Acts 1:8

Energy Level: Medium

Kids will carry the gospel to the ends of the earth in this game to go along with stories about early missionaries.

Divide the room with a line of masking tape. Make one side of the room Jerusalem and the other side Judea. For older children, make the walls of the room Samaria.

Start by having all the children stand on the Jerusalem side of the room, close to the masking tape, with enough room between them so that they won't bump into each other when they jump. Say: **All the disciples started out from Jerusalem, but Jesus told them to take the good news about him to Judea and Samaria and all over the world. Let's pretend we are in Jerusalem now. Across the tape line is Judea. I am going to give each of you a Bible to help you remember that we are taking the good news with us in this game. Listen carefully, and I will tell you when to jump to Judea. Keep listening, because the next time I call out a place, you'll have to jump in the same place if I call out Judea. You'll jump over the line back to Jerusalem if I call out Jerusalem!** Play this game slowly at first, and be sure to alternate calling out Jerusalem and Judea until the kids become comfortable with which area is which. After they have successfully jumped back and forth several times, begin to give directions randomly. When they get really good, introduce Samaria and let them run to touch a wall.

Share Your Square

Supplies: Carpet squares or pieces of paper and a music source

Scripture: Acts 2:42-47

Energy Level: Medium

Demonstrate how early Christians shared with this played-to-music game.

Set out about half as many carpet squares as there are children. Space them far enough apart to have room for the children to walk between them.

Help each child find a partner. Say: **The first Christians learned to share what they had with each other. We're going to play a game like Musical Chairs, but you each will have to share a carpet square with a friend. When the music plays, dance around the squares holding hands as partners. When the music stops, quickly find a carpet square to sit on together.**

Begin the music, and stop it intermittently. After the children have found carpet squares to sit on a couple of times, add variety and adventure to the game by removing one square. Then pairs must share. Tell the kids they don't have to sit on the square and they don't have to have both feet on the square, they only have to touch the square in some way. Remove only as many squares as your preschoolers can comfortably handle.

Chariot Tag

Supplies: None

Scripture: Acts 8:26-40

Energy Level: High

Children will pretend to be chariots in this fast game of Tag.

Ask for one volunteer to be Philip. Say: **The Bible tells us about a man named Philip who ran after a man in his chariot to tell him about Jesus. Today** (child's name) **will be Philip. The rest of you will get down on your hands and knees and crawl around the room on all fours like chariots. When Philip tags you, sit down and wait until all of the other chariots have been tagged. We'll choose a new Philip and play several times.**

Saul's Sight

Supplies: A flashlight

Scripture: Acts 9:1-19

Energy Level: Medium

Emphasize the importance of stopping to listen to God in this game that recalls the story of Saul's conversion.

Have the children stand against one wall in your play area. Stand at the other end with the flashlight. Say: **When Saul saw the bright light from heaven, he fell to the ground and listened to God. I have a bright light in my hand. When you see it turn on, drop to the ground and close your eyes. Then listen for instructions. When I say "go," open your eyes, stand up, and do exactly what you heard me say to do.** Turn off the flashlight as you say "go."

Give the children directions such as "take two backward steps before you walk ahead," "hop on one foot," "crawl forward," or "wiggle as you walk." When one child reaches you, have him or her help you with the flashlight. Send the rest of the children back to begin the game again. Say: **Just as you stopped to listen to me, it's important to take time from what we're doing to stop and listen for God's directions.**

Dorcas Relay

Supplies: None

Scripture: Acts 9:36-43

Energy Level: Medium

Kids will help each other up in this unique partner-relay focusing on the healing of Dorcas.

Have half of the children go to one side of the room and half go to the other side. Have one side of the room be seated (the Dorcas team) and one side remain standing (the Peter team). In this relay, one child from the Peter team will run across the room and take a child who is sitting down by the hand, help him or her up, and then the two will run back across the room together to tap the next player. While the two children are crossing the room, have the rest of the children say, "Dorcas, God has made you well!" Play until all the children on the Dorcas team have been "healed."

Friends Work Together

Supplies: Items to make a simple obstacle course

Scripture: Acts 13

Energy Level: Medium

Kids will journey with partners through thick and thin in this game to accompany the story of Paul and Barnabas' missionary journey.

Set up a simple obstacle course using readily available items such as chairs, pillows, and ropes. You can make a pillow "mountain" to climb over or mark off a "river" to cross with ropes. A row of chairs can become a row of trees to go in and out of. Help the children get into pairs and ask partners to hold hands.

Say: **Friends like Paul and Barnabas work together. You and your partner are like Paul and Barnabas in this game. You have to hold hands and work together no matter what happens.**

Walk through the course to show the kids what to do at each obstacle.

Say: **As long as your hands are together, you can keep going through the course. If you drop hands for any reason, you must start over at the beginning. But you are not in a race. Every pair who makes it to the end with their hands still held together is a winner.**

You can add a different dimension to this game by thinking up silly activities for the partners to do while holding hands. For example, ask the pairs to hop like bunnies while holding hands or have them pretend to shake like jelly.

Lydia's Purple

Supplies: A purple scarf, towel, or length of fabric about three feet long

Scripture: Acts 16:11-15

Energy Level: Medium

Purple fabric helps children visualize Lydia's creations.

Have the children stand in a line about three feet apart. Show the children the purple fabric. Ask: **Have you ever seen someone shake a towel or blanket to get it smooth so it can be folded?** Say: **As we remember the story of Paul and his friend Lydia, we are going to pass the purple to each other in that way. When it's your turn to pass, lift your arms up high and then lower them quickly so that the other end of the fabric flies toward the next person in line. The next person will grab the end of the fabric as it is in the air. Then both of you together will hold it straight out so we can all admire it!** Demonstrate what you want the children to do, and teach them the following verse so that they can all say it together:

> **Lydia, Lydia,**
> **Paul's kind friend,**
> **Pass the purple to** (child's name)
> **By the ends.**

When the fabric is held out, encourage the children to "ooh" and "aah" and say words of admiration! Then have the child who grabbed the end pass the fabric to the next child in line. Continue in this manner until each child has had a turn.

Shake, Shake, Shake the Jail House

Supplies: A music source

Scripture: Acts 16:16-40

Energy Level: High

This game is a perfect follow-up for the story of Paul and Silas in jail.

Designate two children to be Paul and Silas. Have the rest of the children make a prison by standing in a circle and holding hands. Have Paul and Silas stand inside the circle.

Say: **In this Bible story, God used an earthquake to shake the jail where Paul and Silas were prisoners. Let's pretend that this circle is the jail house. When the music begins, Paul and Silas are going to go to each of the jail doors (between your hands) and knock on them. When the music stops, we'll say, "Rumble, rumble, rumble; shake, shake, shake. Here comes a mighty, mighty big earthquake!" Then let go of each other's hands, raise them into the air, and shake them. While everyone is shaking their hands in the air, Paul and Silas will walk around inside the circle and each trade places with someone. Then we will begin the game again with the new Paul and Silas.**

Before beginning the game, the teacher should pretend to be Paul or Silas and demonstrate what they should do. Play until everyone has had a turn.

Needle-and-Thread Relay

Supplies: A length of soft rope or yarn for each group and a chair for each group

Scripture: Acts 18:1-3

Energy Level: Medium

Keep your preschoolers in "stitches" as they play this giant sewing game.

Have the children stand in a single line. If you have more than ten children, form equal groups. Place a chair in front of each group. Instruct children in each group to stand in a straight line in front of their group's chair.

Say: **Just like Paul's needle and thread went in and out as he sewed his tents, you are going to sew in and out for this relay race.**

Say: **First we tie a knot in the end of the thread!** Anchor one end of each group's rope or yarn by tying it to the group's chair. Say: **Then we thread the needle.** Hand the other end of the rope or yarn to the first child in each group. Demonstrate how the first child should carry the rope in front of the next person and then around behind that person. The child will repeat this sequence, zigzagging around each member of the team as though he or she is making stitches through fabric. Then have the child take the stitches out by going through the line in reverse. When the child reaches the front of the line, he or she should pass the rope to the next person and then walk back to the end of the line. The next person will repeat the process.

If you have young preschoolers, have them each pretend to be your needle and guide each one through the "fabric" by the shoulders.

Battered Boat

Supplies: None, but play in a large room with at least one wall cleared of all obstacles (a gym space is best).

Scripture: Acts 27:13-26

Energy Level: High

Play this unique action game when you tell the story of Paul and the stormy sea.

In the middle of the room, have the kids form a large circle and hold hands.

Say: **In this Bible story, Paul was on a boat when a terrible storm came. Let's pretend that we are that boat in the middle of the storm.**

Have the kids walk toward the wall, still holding hands in a circle, until their boat circle touches a wall. Now the storm begins, and the boat begins to roll. Starting with the first child whose back touches the wall, rotate the entire circle so that each child's back touches the wall individually as they move across the wall. When they get to the corner of the room, help the boat move through the sea (open space) again until it touches the next wall. Then the giant wave begins again.

Try singing while the circle is moving through the center of the room as an added twist to this game. Sing the following to the tune of "Row, Row, Row Your Boat":

Row, row, row your boat
in the stormy sea.
Merrily, merrily, merrily, merrily,
Jesus is with me.

Shipwreck!

Supplies: A ball

Scripture: Acts 27

Energy Level: Medium

Your children will enjoy this variation of Hot Potato.

Have the children sit in a circle and pass a ball around the circle. When you call out: **Shipwreck!** the person holding the ball should stand up and jump out of the circle as though he or she is bailing out into the stormy sea. Give the ball to the person next to him or her. Play continues until all the children have bailed out.

Penny Pitch

Supplies: Pennies and an offering basket

Scripture: 2 Corinthians 9:6-7

Energy Level: Low

Use this game as a fun way to give an offering when you learn about Paul's teaching about giving.

Say: **God wants us to give to him with smiles on our faces. Today we will give our offering to God in a fun way. I'll put the basket over here and let each of you toss your coins into the basket, one at a time.** Be sure to give extra pennies to the children who did not bring an offering so that everyone will have a chance to play. The distance you set the basket away from your children depends on their ages. Keep it simple and fun.

The Warmth of Kindness

Supplies: A beanbag for each child and a music source

Scripture: Ephesians 4:32

Energy Level: Medium

Children help friends in this game of balance and kindness.

Give each child a beanbag to balance on the tops of their hands (so that they can't grasp it). Tell the kids that you are going to turn on the music and they can move any way they want to while balancing the beanbags on their hands. If a child drops a beanbag, he or she must freeze until another child picks up the dropped beanbag and replaces it on the first child's hands without dropping his or her own beanbag. If the second child drops his or her beanbag, they are both frozen. If both beanbags are in place, both children are thawed and ready to continue. Turn off the music periodically and have the children freeze. Then tell them to balance their beanbags on their heads, on one finger, or other creative places.

Who Can Do All Things?

Supplies: None

Scripture: Philippians 4:13

Energy Level: Low

Grow kids' confidence through this game of affirmation.

This game uses the same rhythm pattern as "Who Stole the Cookies?" Use these words:

Whole Group: "Who can do all things through Lord Jesus Christ?

(Child's name) can do all things through Lord Jesus Christ!"

Child: "Who, me?" *(Kids can clap two times.)*

Whole Group: "Yes, you!" *(Kids can clap two times.)*

Child: "Yes, I!" *(Kids can clap two times.)*

Whole Group: "And who?"

The first child named chooses another child in the group and the chant repeats. Play until each child is named.